The Story

of

Sidney

Y0-BZZ-128

Bill Landy, a driver for the "Flying Line" motor stage which bussed people to and from Victoria throughout the 1920'.

The Story
of
Sidney

Peter Grant

Porthole Press

Victoria, British Columbia
Canada

1998

Copyright © 1998 Peter Grant

Printed in Canada

Published by Porthole Press Ltd.,
2832 Heath Drive,
Victoria, BC   V9A 2J5
Canada

Canadian Cataloguing in Publication Data

Grant, Peter, 1948-
  The story of Sidney

  ISBN 0-919931-28-6

  1. Sidney (B.C.)--History. I. Title.
FC3849.S52G72 1998   971.1'28   C98-910136-3
F1089.5.S52G72 1998

All rights reserved. No part of this publication may be reproduced,
stored in a retrieval system or transmitted in any form or by any
means, electronic, mechanical, photocopied, recorded or otherwise,
without the prior permission of the copyright owner.

Contents

The foot of Beacon Avenue, viewed from the southeast, about 1895. At L is the Sidney Hotel, on the corner of Beacon and First Street. Sidney quickly became the business centre of North Saanich, with the hotel, a general store (at centre), a butcher and a blacksmith following the sawmill into existence in short order. The hotel burned down in 1948.

Sidney's northern coastline from the air in the 1950s. Above the Beacon Avenue wharf, middle R, is forested Roberts Point, with Roberts Bay beyond, and Armstrong Point the next forested prominence. Beyond it Tsehum (Shoal) Harbour lies, its south shore within the Town of Sidney, the rest in the District of North Saanich.

Introduction

Southeastern Vancouver Island is surrounded by the west coast coniferous forest and ringed by mountains, but in places its rainshadow climate is sunny and dry enough to support the growth of cactus. Sidney occupies a particularly favoured such spot on the east side of the Saanich Peninsula.

First Nation villages preceded European settlement there by at least three thousand years. The Saanich people fished in a territory stretching to British Columbia's mainland shores. Some time before Europeans began to arrive, the band moved across the narrow peninsula to escape raiding by northern tribes – the human cost of living on the busy waterways of Haro Strait was high! The area we call Sidney was settled by farmers after 1862, and in 1891 a family little inclined to farm converted their waterfront land to a railhead townsite.

Incorporated in 1952, Sidney is today a burgeoning town of 11,000 people, having grown tenfold over the last fifty years. While the descendents of pioneering families live there still, Sidney's economic life is now based on transport services, marine recreation and residential lifestyle.

Geography has molded Sidney's character as a transportation hub. The town occupies just 714 hectares (1764 acres), less than a sixth of the size of the neighbouring District of North Saanich, but it sits on a fateful spot between Tsehum Harbour and Patricia Bay, on a flat prairie barely 2 kilometres (1.2 miles) wide. People bound for Victoria (metro population, including Sidney: 313,000) typically land on Vancouver Island at the huge BC Ferries terminal at Swartz Bay and cross this prairie on Route 17, the Patricia Bay Highway.

Since 1960 the highway has become the major artery between Victoria and B.C.'s population centre, Vancouver, with nearly two million residents. Further south, Mt. Newton forms a natural boundary between North and Central Saanich and squeezes the traffic eastward into a narrow corridor. In 1967, Sidney enlarged its boundaries to embrace the highway.

A much smaller terminal in town links Vancouver Island and the U.S.A., via the San Juan Islands, using routes to Anacortes, Wa. that originated in the 1920s. The Victoria International Airport is a third port of entry and the connector to flights in and out of Vancouver International Airport.

The climate is another prime influence on Sidney's character. Staff at the airport's meteorology station have kept the official Victoria weather records for more than 50 years. Average annual sunshine totals 2080 hours — just slightly the most sunny place in the vast province of British Columbia (area 950,000 square kilometres / 366,000 sq miles). Annual rainfall totals just 880 millimetres (34.6 inches), almost the driest place on the west coast of Canada.

The light-giving sun attracted an agricultural research station that has operated for more than 75 years. Like the airport, the station is a neighbour and friend of Sidney and thus part of Sidney's story. More importantly, the climate has drawn people to settle in Sidney in numbers.

Sidney's coastline and marine surroundings are the third key factor in its makeup. South of Beacon Avenue stretches the simple shore of Bazan Bay, where the little prairie runs straight into the ocean. To the north, the coast becomes rocky, cliffy, deeply indented. Numerous marinas are tucked into the folds of Tsehum Harbour and nearby coves, sheltering thousands of pleasure and commercial craft. Sidney is the prime jumping-off point for the many clusters of reefs and little islands that poke above the swirling tides of Haro Strait.

Sidney is a hard-working community — always has been. Less than a lifespan ago Sidney had a smokestack economy, with a port bustling with ferries and industrial vessels and a businesslike waterfront studded with docks. A whistle blew and Sidney's few streets filled with workers from the cannery, the sawmill, a roofing plant. Fishers returned from trolling in little boats amid the islands. Dairy farmers and orchardists drove into the little town on prairie backroads. Chauffeured limos would embark from fine homes hidden along Sidney's northern waterfront.

Sidney's charmingly eccentric agricultural history runs to duck farming, kelp farming and pear farming. Its vanished industries include a ships' boiler descaling compound, manufactured in a family-run backyard Sidney factory for two generations and distributed around the world. From Sidney's career in transportation come tales of the hapless, short-lived but ever-so-colourful Victoria and Sidney Railway and SS *Iroquois*.

People reinvent themselves and so do communities. Individuals point their feet away from the past to find new homes or build new careers. In adapting to changing circumstances, communities sometimes start over, too. Buildings that seemed as secure as the mountains are razed.

Sidney is a community that has reinvented itelf not once but again and again, on the same site. To put the same thought another way, most of the material culture represented in this book is gone, and what remains of the Sidney of yesteryear is fast disappearing.

This book traces the fortunes of this fascinating place through photograph and story. It is intended to conjure up the flavours of Sidney's bygone days, not to be a definitive work. The photographs are arranged to illustrate the dominant themes of Sidney's history. Sidney has its share of good stories, and I am indebted to its citizens and writers for sharing their knowledge and perspective.

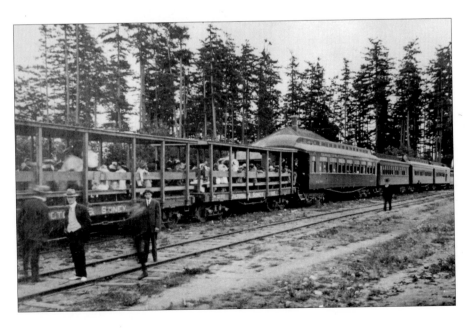

Seated figure holding a dish, from North Saanich, at the Field Museum, Chicago, 1901. Three of these ancient sculptures, perhaps 2000 years old, were found at Tsehum (Shoal) Harbour sites in 1898 and 1899, while anthropologist Harlan Smith was studying burial cairns. "Practically every cove in the shores of North Saanich Bay (Shoal Harbour) has its shell heap marking the site of an ancient village," Smith wrote, "and cairns were found on nearly every promontory." The eminent ethnologist Franz Boas visited the site. The seated figures originated in ancient centres on the Fraser River. Their use in initiation rituals was detailed by BC Provincial (now Royal BC) Museum ethnologist Wilson Duff in his 1975 book Images: Stone: BC.

1. Before Sidney

Long before there was a town called Sidney, people lived in the vicinity. Artifacts recovered from the Sidney area date to the Locarno Beach Period, perhaps 3000 years ago. (After the Fraser Glaciation, the sea level on the B.C. coast rose and fell considerably, stabilizing near the present shoreline about 5000 years ago.) The remains of many ancient villages ring Tsehum (Shoal) Harbour, on Sidney's north coast, and there is more evidence of occupation around Bazan Bay.

Figures in a canoe, found on a North Saanich property in 1969. The mysterious figures, possibly part of an old burial monument, may be connected to some ritual site or activity associated, perhaps, with sea mammal hunting.

Less than two centuries ago a large winter village of the Northern Straits Salish First Nations stood on Tsehum Harbour. The village was smitten by smallpox towards the end of the 18th century and suffered a drastic loss in population, according to a 1940 study of the Saanich people by anthropologist Diamond Jenness, who wrote, "During the first half of the 19th century the old village near Sidney that has since disappeared contained six and probably more big houses, each of which sheltered several families."

Tseycum village on Patricia Bay in 1917. "In the early 1890s," anthropologist Wayne Suttles recorded in 1951, "there were four old-style houses here, one of hewn wall planks and a plank shed roof, the other three of lumber and shakes. The owner of the older house was dead; the owners of the other three were Harry, Jim and two brothers, Jack and Pierre. Each owned reef-net locations at Point Roberts [near Tsawwassen on the mainland shore]; therefore all or nearly all of the settlement went there for the [salmon] fishing season."

Another threat took the form of night-time raids by bands of the Comox or Kwakiutl people who paddled down the coast every Spring. "The Saanich Indians," Jenness wrote, "sent their women and children to secluded spots during May and June, the usual season for raids, while the men maintained a nightly watch on the housetops."

Old Katie, an ancient resident of Tseycum village, photographed in 1934. She was born about 1827 in a Salish village on the lower Fraser River, married Chief Jim of Saanich and moved to his home, the middle one in the photo opposite. When the Saanich Nation signed a treaty with Vancouver Island Governor James Douglas at Deep Cove in 1852, she was there.

Katie had a long association with the North Saanich farming community. "It was said she ran the first second hand shop from her home in Patricia Bay," The Daily Colonist *related. "She was washerwoman for several families and she performed her chores in bare feet, but wearing several hats."*

Moran Brethour recalls her visits to his grandfather Julius's home. She would open the back door and enter, take out dishes reserved for her alone and have lunch, all in silence, sitting at a table by herself. Then she and Julius would converse in Chinook, the coastal trading jargon.

Old Katie died in 1934.

Fishing/hunting canoe at Tsawout village, on Saanichton Bay, south of Sidney, 1923. Such vessels were likely in daily use. Fishing or sea mammal hunting gear visible in the two-person craft include a seal-skin float, harpoon lines and shafts and rush mats to sit on.

The Saanich First Nation continued to hunt ducks in the old manner in Tsehum Harbour as late as 1912. This picture, by resident Francis Barrow, shows hunters in a line of boats beyond the North Saanich wharf.

At some point during the 19th century the band dwindled to such an extent they took decisive action, Jenness's study relates: "The Saanich abandoned their village near Sidney, on the east side of the peninsula, and moved to Patricia Bay, on the west side, where they were less exposed to attack. The Sidney village was known as Sai'klam, 'clay,' and Patricia Bay was called Klangan 'salty place;' but when the Sidney inhabitants moved over to Patricia Bay they transferred the name 'Clay' to their new home." The present name of the reserve on Patricia Bay, Tseycum, does indeed seem to echo the name Tsehum Harbour, across the prairie.

In 1846 a boundary commission established the 49th parallel N as the border between the United States and British territories. A treaty affirmed the British claim to Vancouver Island. In 1849 the entire 32,000-square-kilometre island was leased to the Hudson's Bay Company for seven shillings a year, subject to its establishing a colony in short order. Governor James Douglas concluded treaties with the Salish Nations between Victoria and Nanaimo and with the Kwakiutl Nation of Fort Rupert. The Saanich Nation was consigned to three village reserves and smaller ones on the Gulf Islands.

Sidney's pioneers were drawn to British Columbia during Gold Rush days, beginning in 1858. From the decks of sternwheelers and sailing ships plying the busy straits from Fort Victoria to the gold fields at Yale or the camel trains at Harrison Lake, they watched the green and gold Saanich Peninsula slide by. Some vowed to return.

A year after the Fraser River gold rush began, a colonial proclamation established pre-emptive land sales for farmers. Few families rushed to settle on the Saanich Peninsula and much of North Saanich was initially acquired by speculators.

The threat of First Nations raiding parties initially scared settlers away from areas exposed to the straits. The threat soon subsided. Raids on Saanich villages by Kwakiutl had already ceased by 1862, when a disastrous smallpox epidemic reduced coastal First Nations populations by one-third.

HMS Plumper

The 1846 Treaty of Washington established the British territorial boundary with the United States but left uncertain the ownership of the San Juan Islands, part of the archipelago between the straits of Georgia (to the north) and Juan de Fuca (south). The treaty specified only that the border follow the middle of the channel separating Vancouver Island from the mainland. A boundary commission was established in 1857 to adjudicate a settlement. Enter HMS *Plumper*, a 484-ton steam sloop bearing a Royal Navy surveying party, posted to the Pacific coast for three years beginning in November 1857 to continue Captain Vancouver's work (1792-94) charting the vast coastline. "A routine was established," *British Columbia Chronicle* relates, "whereby from March to November the *Plumper* was usually at sea despatching parties in small boats to the work inshore. From November until March the *Plumper* was at her base in Esquimalt, where a drafting office was set up in one of the 'Crimea huts.' Here the observations of the preceding field season were converted into charts for forwarding to England."

Captain (later Admiral and Sir) George Richards, standing 3rd from L, with Mrs. Richards and surveying officers of HMS Plumper, including, seated from L: Sub-Lieutenant Edward P. Bedwell, 2nd Lieut. Richard C. Mayne and 1st Lieut. William Moriarty; standing from L: William B. Wood (surgeon), William Brown (paymaster) and Lieut. Daniel Pender (at R).

The party spent the summer of 1859 in the waters of Haro Strait, then a hot-spot because of rival American and British claims to possession of the San Juan Islands. Most of the coastal features in the Sidney area, including Sidney Island and the Canadian Gulf Islands, were named by Richards. The party continued surveying until 1868. Richards returned home, and Pender took command of Beaver, the pioneering HBC coastal steamer, to complete (1871) the survey of all the British Columbia coastline to 54 degrees 40 minutes N latitude. The San Juan dispute almost led to armed conflict in 1859. Both countries garrisoned the islands until the rival claims to ownership were adjudicated by the German Kaiser in 1872. A compromise solution was rejected, and the islands were awarded to the United States in their entirety.

Sidney Island from the south

The town of Sidney, named after Sidney Island, commemorates a person who likely never set foot on North American soil. Earlier known as Sallas (meaning uncertain), Sidney Island was named in 1859 for Frederick William Sidney, Captain Richards' Royal Navy colleague in hydrographic surveying. Sidney's devotion to surveying the New South Wales coast of Australia rivalled Richards' legendarily thorough work in British Columbia.

An item in *The British Colonist*, May 24, 1860: "There was a sale by auction in Victoria, of real estate on Sallas island, offered by the Hudson Bay Company, at the upset price of six shillings an acre. There was a large attendance, but few purchasers. One attendant at the sale wished to know who would defend any settlers on the island from the Indians, and said that for his part he would not give sixpence an acre let alone six shillings. The auctioneeer observed that his remarks were unnecessary and uncalled for. After two or three lots had been sold, the sale was adjourned."

The Right Reverend George Hills, first Anglican Bishop of British Columbia, arrived on Vancouver Island in 1860 with a generous endowment from an English patroness.

He invested some money in land in North Saanich. The entire Saanich Peninsula was marked off in 100 acre lots in 1859 and offered for sale to settlers at 4 shillings halfpenny an acre, with one lot to single settlers, two to couples and fractions for each child. Hills followed the pattern of other speculators who were buying tracts just released from reserve, subdividing and selling off within a few years. For example, in 1869 James Menagh bought 160 acres from Rev. Hills for $640. It is today the south side of Sidney.

It is not recorded that Rev. Hills ever farmed his North Saanich land. Perhaps he toiled in the vineyards of real estate for the Anglican Church? This portrait of Rev. Hills was taken in 1890.

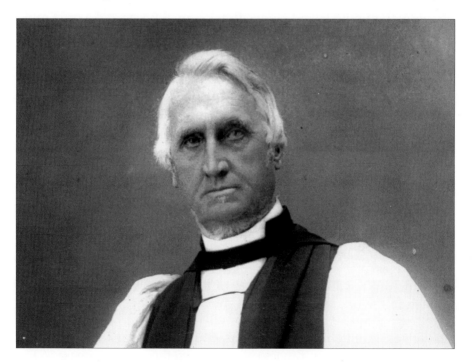

Sidney Pioneers

Richard **John**'s family came out from Wales in 1858 and, according to family history, settled in the area of North Saanich that is now Sidney in 1863. Richard John, pictured here, continued to work the gold fields for 10 years, making annual trips home to 600-acre Glamorgan Farm, which was centred where Sandown Racetrack now stands.

In 1872 John's compatriate Samuel **Roberts**, another gold miner, bought more than 300 acres from the Johns and established Beaufort Farm, on Roberts Bay. He in turn sold 80 acres to his German mining friend Henry **Brackman**, who started a grist mill.

Another of Roberts' mining cronies, Irishman George **Mills**, settled on a farm on the west side, where the airport is now. In 1873 the Donald **McDonald** family, from Scotland, settled on 370 acres on All Bay and Tsehum Harbour, and the Wilson **Armstrong** family started 160-acre Maple Farm, which took in Armstrong Point and Resthaven Island.

The year 1873 is also memorable for the arrival of the **Brethour** family, whose ancestors had migrated from Germany to Ireland and more recently Ontario. Samuel and Margaret Brethour and their children moved onto 500 acres on Haro Strait, south and east of those settlers' farms. South and west of them were the **Reay** brothers, William and Charles, who settled on 1100 acres in 1875 after mining for gold.

Samuel Roberts came to Vancouver Island in 1854. His wife, Agnes Gough, was one of the first children of European origin born at Nanaimo. "We will send one soon of the girls," Agnes wrote on the backing of the original of the print shown top right. "We are going to have some more taken of the mob. Will send some to Uncle John and yourselves. I thought Uncle William would like to see Castle Roberts. That is what he and Mr. Davies called it when they came to see us." The Roberts house, a first building on land now in Sidney, was torn down in 1969.

The Roberts family at their home, built in 1873, south of Roberts Bay.

An early industrial site in North Saanich (1878), and one of British Columbia's first steam-powered grist mills, Henry Brackman's operation on Tsehum (Shoal) Harbour was abandoned after less than two decades – it seems the mill couldn't draw enough water. Brackman Ker Ltd. moved to Victoria and went on to become a giant manufacturer and marketer of rolled oats and flours.

Samuel Brethour and Margaret St. John were both descended from German Palatine families. Married in Ontario in 1844, they had 11 children. Samuel lived only four years after settling in North Saanich; Margaret died in 1883. Their 500 acres, divided among five sons, became the nucleus of the Sidney townsite.

"Janesville Farm, Residence of J. Brethour."
Charmingly depicted, it is inscribed from Brethour to the family of his late wife Jane. This lacquered painting of the John Brethour family farm is dated August 12, 1890. Jane Dowswell, the family history relates, was John's childhood sweetheart from Uxbridge, Ontario. They had five children, and, after her death in 1890, John (1847-1923) remarried and had five more. The farmhouse was torn down in 1947 to make way for airport expansion. The picture, by an itinerant painter, hangs in the Saanich Pioneer Society's log cabin in Saanichton.

North Saanich School was the first established in the district, in 1873, in the Institute Hall, which Donald McDonald and others built on Mills Road. Henry Brethour was the first teacher. Pictured here is the class of 1906, with teacher James Monk.

The first church built in the vicinity of present-day Sidney was the North Saanich Methodist Church, built 1891 at Mills and the East Road. It was demolished in the 1930s.

Ah Sing, a farm worker at the John family's Aberavon Farm, North Saanich, photgraphed in 1880. Few photographs document the enormous role of Asian workers in the life of Sidney, whether on farms, in the sawmill or in commercial fishing.

23

2. Sidney Invented

Some towns seem to grow out of the earth overnight like mushrooms. Sidney was one of these instant communities. Unlike places in British Columbia that owe their existence to mining or railway interests, Sidney was invented, when the Brethours pooled their 100-acre farms, surveyed a townsite, started selling lots, and concluded negotiations for a 16-mile railway to Victoria.

The terminus stimulated the establishment of a busy port. Families built homes and put down roots. A fully-functioning town evolved. By contrast, Crofton, another Vancouver Island instant town of the same era housed copper smelter workers and their families. When the smelter closed, the town languished.

How did the Brethour brothers succeed? Good location, for one. They beat out the Brackman Ker - Roberts interests, which proposed that the railway terminus be at the North Saanich wharf on Tsehum (Shoal) Harbour. They also recognized the need for an industrial base and exploited the value of the attractive waterfront setting and the sunny climate in getting a community going. Throw a bit of romance into the bargain, too – it helped to get a sawmill up and running! The mill, built on land donated by the Brethours, operated for nearly half a century, and its dry sheds remained on Beacon Avenue for decades longer as a lumber store.

A railway was first proposed for the Saanich Peninsula in 1879. A rail port on the peninsula, the thinking went, would enable railcars to be put onto barges for towing across Georgia Strait. Victoria would become a transcontinental terminus, of sorts. A charter obtained by politician Amor de Cosmos was narrowly defeated on a by-law vote in Victoria.

When the Irvings, a Victoria shipping family, went partners with the Brethours in the Victoria and Sidney Railway in 1892, it was intended simply to provide access to market for the products of the peninsula. Public money underwrote the operation.

A V & S passenger train at the Sidney station in its first year of operation. Julius Brethour, a member of the railway's first board of directors, poses at centre. To his right is conductor Andy Forbes, renowned for his unfailing courtesy even under fire by irate passengers on a hot train stalled in the countryside. The tender is filled with the wood fuel that earned the line the nickname The Cordwood Limited. Engineer Dave Hasker is in the cab.

The Sidney railway station on a summer morning.

From the antiquated spark-catcher funnel of old Engine #1 to the open-sided "cattle-cars" passengers sometimes had to be content with, it was a laughable affair. As a railway terminus Sidney lasted less than 30 years. V&S passenger service often ran hours late and sometimes not at all. This situation was documented in the fulminations of Sir Clive Phillips-Wolley of Piers Island in letters to *The Daily Colonist*.

The little line was bought by the Great Northern Railway in 1902. Things didn't improve, though it generated freight business across Georgia Strait and up the east coast of Vancouver Island.

One of the enduring figures in the town's history is the jaunty *S.S. Iroquois*. In the early years of this century, it regularly served dozens of landings between Sidney and Nanaimo. After it went down in 1911, Sidney remained a transport centre for the Canadian Gulf Islands. When the highway took over from steel and steam, the ferry trade to the American shore developed, and Sidney enjoyed a long and vigorous span as a regional port. Ferries bulk large in Sidney's history.

SS Iroquois *docked at Fulford Harbour, on Salt Spring Island, about 1910. The wooden-sided* Iroquois *began service in 1900, was 82 feet in length and weighed 195 tons loaded. The company soon picked up the mail contract for the Gulf Islands. Beetling around between Sidney and Nanaimo until 1911, it competed successfully with the Dunsmuir family's coastal shipping line.*

A Brethour family gathering: from L, brothers Samuel, Jr., Henry, Wesley, John and Julius Brethour, with their spouses: Annie (Mrs. Sam), Magdelene (Mrs. Julius), Deborah (John's second partner), Jennie (Mrs. Wesley) and, in front, Alotta (Henry's second wife and sister of J.J. White).

The Brethour property extended from the water to the East Road (about where the long runway begins at the airport) on either side of Beacon Avenue. John's 100-acre share was the southernmost, and the next was owned by Julius, then those of Wesley, Henry and Samuel, Jr.

"John was the only true farmer of the family," writes Moran Brethour, and he "kept his farm intact." His waterfront was later the site of the Sidney Rubber Roofing plant, and in the upland was a little subdivision called The Orchard.

Julius, the driving force behind the V&S Railway, granted his waterfront to the railway for "dockage, station and other facilities." Wesley "was more of a builder," with "ventures in Victoria."

Henry and the eldest brother, William, went east. Henry returned to take up the land of the seventh brother, Philip, who died in 1883 of typhoid fever. (Their mother, Margaret, died three days later.) Henry and Wesley gave up the waterfront portion of their lands for the mill.

Samuel, Jr.'s interests included farming, mining and the operation of the V&S.

Picnic at J.J. White's camp on Shell (Ker) Island, White standing at right.

"John White, an ex-politician and distant relative of the Brethours," Moran Brethour writes, "came west from Ontario looking for opportunities for some Toronto investors, and he suggested that, with certain incentives, his group would start a sawmill to supply the needs for railroad construction, plus the needs of an expected real estate boom that the railroad would create."

Soon John's nephew James Johnston White came out from Ontario, too. He met and courted Stella (Caroline Estelle), eldest daughter of Henry Brethour.

The Whites' consortium built the mill and made J.J. the foreman. It provided the ties and lumber for the railroad, then went broke. White later admitted the closest he'd been to lumbering was living in a riverside town with an annual log drive!

He was appointed Sidney station agent for the railway and customs officer for the port, a job he held until 1934. As a partner in the Sidney Trading Company and co-founder of the Saanich Canning Company, White was a pillar of Sidney's economy.

When Sidney incorporated in 1952, White was elected the first chairman of commissioners (mayor) at age 84.

Clive Phillips-Wolley (1854-1918), a sometime lawyer, a widely-published poet and essayist of Empire and an ardent British Imperialist, was knighted in 1914 for services to the Crown, including establishment of a local branch of the Navy League. Sir Clive's collected poems, Songs from a Young Man's Land, *were published in 1917. Clive and his expatriate British family built a fine house in Oak Bay, near Victoria, but it wasn't far enough away from the hurly-burly, so they setted on Piers Island, about 7 km (4 mi) north of Sidney, in 1901. They were the sole residents of the island until moving to Somenos, near Duncan, in 1909. In Phillips-Wolley's many letters to* The Daily Colonist *during his residence on Piers Island, he often referred to the V&S Railway as the CPR — the Creeping Paralysis Railway.*

Bazan Bay, looking northeast from the Dominion Experimental Farm, with Sidney in the distance at L. By 1917 three railway lines — V&S, British Columbia Electric and Canadian Northern Pacific — puffed and rattled across the lowland strip in the middle distance. The Patricia Bay Highway, the major approach to Victoria, now occupies the same corridor. The V&S right-of-way is now Lochside Drive.

The Toronto and British Columbia Milling and Manufacturing Company was awarded 30-year timber leases on more than 16 000 hectares (nearly 40,000 acres) of forestland on the west coast of Vancouver Island as a timber supply for the mill. The Sidney mill's first quarter century was clouded by economic depression. It was closed more than it operated and hardly worked its holdings. After many changes of name and owner, it stabilized under the management of G.H. Walton and the name Sidney Mills in 1917. Until forced out of business in the Great Depression, the mill was the mainstay of the community, converting big logs into lumber.

Sidney Mills Company employees, 1921 or 1922, during the mill's heyday.
The mill's workforce was estimated as high as 325.

Logs were towed to mill in long rafts by steam tugs, usually after cable yarding with steam "donkeys" and transported to tidewater by geared steam Shay or Climax locomotives. At the mill the logs were cut with steam saws. The Sidney mill had a 5-foot-radius steam-powered circular head saw.

The mill put out plenty of smoke, too. A big burner on the waterfront was fed a steady diet of sawdust, cuttings, odds and ends. After the Great War a giant brick smokestack attached to the power plant marked Sidney's skyline. In those days billowing black smoke and its sooty fallout were good — they meant business, work, pay.

Chinese and East Indian men comprised a high proportion of the millworkers.

Logs in the water beside the Sidney sawmill, inside a small breakwater that has become part of the infill for the Port of Sidney development.

Mitchell and Anderson, Beacon Avenue and Second Street 1981. Originally the mill's lumber storage shed, the corner housed the mill office during its latter years. When the mill closed forever in 1934, it continued as a lumber sales centre until razed to make way for the Landmark Building in 1981.

SS Strathcona *and the V&S train at Sidney, 1902. The railway wharf was just south of the Government Wharf, built the same year at the foot of Beacon Avenue. The* Strathcona, *a sternwheeled riverboat, incongruously appeared on the Sidney–Nanaimo route. Here, the waiting southbound train meets the just-docked sternwheeler. Interminable waits at train stations along the line could be traced to late-arriving boats and the vagaries of Gulf Islands traffic and tides. The ship blew a cylinder late in 1902 and was taken off the route.*

The east end of Beacon Avenue about 1910. The Canadian Pacific Railway steamer Queen City *is at the Government Dock, the SS* Iroquois *at the V&S dock. The Hotel Sidney is at right. The train tracks (foreground) entered the mill site off L.*

David John's family and Ah Sing (at right), haying, 1890s.

North Saanich Hotel (Wright's Hotel), Toketie (Mill) Point, near the North Saanich Wharf. Originally the warehouse of the Saanich Steam Mill, the building housed the district's first post ofice and store and was converted to a hotel in 1892, which went out of business in 1906. The district's commercial activity had already shifted to the new town of Sidney. The building was torn down in 1915.

Tug Constance near Sidney, 1895. Such vessels played a prominent role in the young town's commerce. In 1902, Great Northern Railway (GNR) bought the V&S and the next year started a railcar barge service between Sidney and its mainland railhead at Liverpool, opposite New Westminster, as well as a combined railcar and ferry system between Sidney and Port Guichon, near Ladner. The passenger service didn't last. Tugs kept towing railcar barges out of Sidney until 1919.

SS Iroquois went aground in a thick fog near Nanaimo in late Octover 1908. The little ship sank with the falling tide. Underwater carpenters sealed off the holds and cabins and pumped out the water, and in no time it was afloat again

The End of the Iroquois

"Short and stubby... stands an enormous distance out of the water... might be top-heavy in a rough sea," the *Nanaimo Daily Herald* wrote of the SS *Iroquois* after her first trip to Nanaimo on April 2, 1900.

The words proved a terrible understatement. On April 10, 1911, the *Iroquois* foundered shortly after leaving Sidney in a southeastly gale. The little ship had two decks, and she was carrying unsecured cargo, including bar iron, on the open upper deck, while the cargohold was left unballasted. A.D. Munro, the ship's purser and co-owner of the Sidney and Nanaimo Transportation Company with *Iroquois* captain Albert Sears, is said to have noted the stiffening wind and told a passenger, "If the cargo shifts, we're lost."

The cargo did shift. In a vicious gust, the *Iroquois* heeled over, the cargo shifted, and the ship wouldn't right. The top and bottom separated and it went down before making Roberts Bay, while the whole town watched. One lifeboat swamped with nine passengers aboard. 21 people died, including 14 passengers and purser Munro. Ten people survived, six in the ship's employ, including Captain Sears. The six were in a lifeboat which, although staved in, made it to Curteis Point. Sears then went home.

Meanwhile, braving the storm, George Brethour raced his launch to the site with Jim McArthur, but the steering gear broke and they lost precious time. Three Cowichan First Nation men clamming on Sidney Island also rushed to the rapidly sinking ship and saved four lives. More were rescued in vain. Some died in people's parlours, under doctor's care, of the effects of hypothermia.

A coroner's inquest and a manslaughter trial followed. The *Iroquois's* rapid sinking was judged to have been hastened by having ordinary glass in the lower deck windows. Sears was held responsible for the unstowed cargo on the upper deck and for not staying with the ship longer. Admiralty Court ruled that the right thing for Sears to have done would have been to take to the life boats and remain "attached to and under the lea of" the sinking ship as long as possible.

Sears was aquitted of manslaughter and pointedly exonerated for his actions after reaching shore, but he lost his Master's licence. He had already been judged, harshly, by the community.

On the urging of the trial judge, the three First Nations rescuers, William Tzouhalem, Bob Klutzwhalen and Donat Charlie, were awarded medals for bravery by the Government of Canada.

Barge at Sidney loaded with clam shells, bound for Bellingham, Washington. Jim White started a back-room clam cannery in 1903, the first on the coast to pack clams in their own nectar. The Saanich Canning Company soon branched into fruit and vegetables. Standing on the barge are White and C.C. Cochran, partners in this important Sidney industry, which shipped the peninsula's products to distant markets until the 1940s.

Workers in the Saanich Canning plant at the foot of Beacon Avenue, 1930.

Sidney fisherman Manuel Seglabra would cast his nets the old Portugese way, a little ways off shore, Moran Brethour recalls.

The buildings were torn down in the 1950s.

Ralph Marshall hauling a truckload of firewood, Bazan Bay brickyard, about 1930. Local blue clay was the chief ingredient of the high-quality soft mud bricks, tiles and flower pots that were manufactured here for decades and at the Bazan Bay Brick and Tile Company beginning in 1919. Another brickyard operated on Sidney Island.

Morris Thomas, the first real estate agent in Sidney, clearing land on Portland Island, with his family and an assistant, 1906. Construction of the Panama Canal stimulated a residential building boom on Vancouver Island that lasted until 1913.

The Sidney Rubber Roofing Company made sheet asphalt roofing in a plant constructed along the V&S just south of Sidney in 1913. When the factory burned down in 1921, the company built a new plant on the Songhees reserve in Victoria West.

The Sidneway stop on the Interurban railway. The BC Electric Railway Company, operator of the Victoria streetcar system and various hydroelectric power generators, completed a second railway line on the Saanich Peninsula in 1912, bringing electricity to Sidney. Well-appointed electric parlour cars ran between the city and Deep Bay (Deep Cove), where there was a small hotel (now the renowned Deep Cove Chalet restaurant). The Sidneway stop was more than a mile from town.

Looking west along Beacon Avenue between Second and Third streets, after 1912. In the middle, Critchley's store and post office. Beyond, the Merchants' Bank of Canada, later the Bank of Montreal.

Chinatown, Beacon Avenue, south side, east of Fifth, 1914. The apartments were home for many single Asian men who worked in the mill. The buildings were gone when the mill closed.

In the North Saanich Post Office, beside Critchley's Store, 1912: Alfred Critchley, William Whiting, owner Jim Critchley and, holding a mailbag, postmaster "Doc" Blasson.

The Sidney and Islands Review started publishing in 1912. The presses could be operated by motor or foot-pedal.

The younger generation of North Saanich pioneering families, 1912. L to R: Margaret Michell John Smith, Wilson Armstrong, Norm Armstrong, Jean John, George John.

Emily Jean John (1900-1975) was born on Aberavon, an 80-acre farm that was her parents' wedding gift from her grandparents, Richard John and Ann Graer. Her father was David John (1854-1901) and her mother, Margaret Michell (1866-1951), the daughter of South Saanich pioneers.

Jean lived most of her life at Aberavon with her mother and brother William (1892-1968). "They maintained [a] reputation for generous hospitality to a wide circle of friends and neighbours. They will always be remembered for their fine garden and the generosity with which they shared it. Never a visitor left their house without taking with them a gift of flowers, vegetables, fruit, honey or a loaf of freshly-baked bread" (*Sidney Review*, February 12, 1975).

In 1960 William and Jean moved off the farm. "Been here too long," William confided to Colonist reporter James K. Nesbitt. "If I had my life to live over again I'd move around more." The farmhouse was torn down to make way for the Patricia Bay Highway extension to Swartz Bay. An old grey barn opposite the Chevron Station was all that remained of Aberavon.

Group at the Dominion Experimental Farm, 1912 or 1913.

The experimental farm occupied North Saanich land on either side of the East Road and down to Bazan Bay beginning in 1912. Giant Douglas firs and red cedars were felled to create the farm. Its original purpose was to research the agricultural potential of southeastern Vancouver Island. Over the decades, experimental plantings were established for apples, pears, loganberries and strawberries, as well as figs, persimmons, pomegranates and other exotic fruits; various vegetables; teas; rubber trees; and ornamental hollies, a local winner. An arboretum was established along the upland boundary. Animal husbandry research evolved over the same period. Tree fruit pollination work and greenhouse research came later. Beginning in the 1960s, plant quarantine work and tissue-culture research increasingly occupied the station. Since 1987 it has assumed a national food inspection function. All fruit tree stock and grapevines intended for import to Canada are examined for viral infections there and either allowed, detained or refused entry. The waterfront portion of the experimental farm, cut off by the Patricia Bay Highway in the 1950s, is now Bazan Bay Marine Park (accessible from Lochside Drive), and the present size of the Centre for Plant Health, to use the name adopted in 1996, is about 40 hectares (100 acres).

John Macoun (1831-1920), a prominent Canadian botanist and resident of Sidney from 1912.

As a plant geographer in the 1870s, John Macoun studied the suitability of the dry grasslands of southern Alberta and Saskatchewan for settlement and agricuture, and his optimism about the so-called Palliser Triangle helped swing the Government of Canada towards a southerly route for the Canadian Pacific Railway, with incalculable impact on western Canadian history.

Macoun was Dominion Botanist with the Geological Survey of Canada from 1882 to 1912, and he assembled a national herbarium that included some 1000 species that he discovered and named. The rare Macoun's meadowfoam is one.

His collection of Vancouver Island plants included 826 flowering species, 195 lichens and more than 1,000 mosses, seaweeds and fungi by 1915. He gave a large collection to the Provincial (now Royal B.C.) Museum in 1917.

Prof. Macoun's son James, an associate for nearly 40 years, died a few months before him. In the interval, Macoun wrote a naturalist's column for the Review under the name *Rambler*, inviting readers to send in specimens for identification. His son-in-law, Sidney-area naturalist Arthur O. Wheeler, established the Alpine Club of Canada.

Another son, William T. Macoun, was Dominion Horticulturist and a noted apple breeder. At the experimental farm W.T. Macoun's work is evident in the arboretum and other early plantings.

Amy Barrow and animals

Amy Barrow was a Bradford, a rich and powerful family in Surrey, England. Londoner Francis Barrow visited Vancouver Island for his health and, in 1906, bought the old Brackman-Ker grist mill, the store, the livestock and the 10 acres they stood on. He and Amy married in England and soon settled in North Saanich. The childless couple enjoyed an eccentric, moneyed life at Toketie Point. *Upcoast Summers* chronicles their travels along the vast B.C. coast in "the little ship Toketie" with two cocker spaniels.

Francis was an accomplished amateur archaeologist. He photo-documented coastal First Nation petroglyphs and pictographs and corresponded for decades with archaeologist Harlan Smith, with whom he shared, unfortunately, the habit of disturbing grave sites. Francis died in 1944, Amy in 1962.

Sidney's close relationship with the armed forces began in the years before World War I, when a summer service industry grew up around militia camps.

A number of distinguished men of war were associated with Sidney. One was Victoria Cross winner Col. Cy Peck, who became MLA for the district. Another VC winner, Gen. George Pearkes, married a Sidney woman, Blytha Copeman. Gen. Sir Arthur Currie, field commander of the Canadian Corps during World War I, and now thought to be the Great War's most brilliant tactical leader, was Sidney School's first teacher (1894-95).

A military parade progresses up Beacon Avenue at Second Street, 1912.

"Before war's end the community of Sidney and area, with a population of about 800, would have 200 men serving in the military. In rapid succession, the closure of the mill was followed by the brickyard and other local factories" (*V&S, The Victoria and Sidney Railway*, by Darryl E. Muralt).

Canadian Explosives' plant on James Island, 1916.

James Island lies about 5 kilometres (3 mi) southeast of Sidney and is 316 hectares (780 acres) in size. Canadian Explosives Ltd. bought the entire island and, in 1913, laid out Canada's largest powder manufacturing plant. The plant was adapted to manufacture the powerful new explosive trinitrotoluol (TNT), and the island found itself occupied by 800 workers, some housed initially in tents. At the peak of the Great War the plant produced two million pounds a month of Alfred Nobel's invention, and "large quantities of nitric acid were also produced... as an adjunct to TNT production. A by-product of this was sodium sulphate, urgently needed by the Canadian paper industry and normally bought overseas." (*Looking Back on James Island* by Bea Bond, Porthole Press, Sidney, 1991). Wharves and two little railway lines expedited the delivery of bulk raw materials — "nitrate of soda from Chile; phosphate rock from Florida; glycerine, nitrate of ammonia and potash from Europe; and sulphur from Japan" — and, on the other side of the island, shipment of the deadly products.

A little village evolved at the north end of James Island, where tennis matches on hardwood courts might be interrupted by wandering fallow deer. The TNT plant, converted to dynamite and other explosives and under the name Canadian Industries Ltd. (CIL), supported the village, with its own school, until 1961. Some James Island houses continue in use as Sidney residences. The CIL plant closed forever in 1978.

B Company 1916 parade camp, Sidney. The building in the L background, on Third Street, was known as the House of David, and was a house of ill-repute. David was the owner's surname. The Merchant's Bank, on the corner of Third and Beacon, is at R.

The first airplane known to visit Sidney landed in Wesley Brethour's field in 1919 — a harbinger of North Saanich's destiny as an international airport site.

50

Abandoned Victoria and Sidney Railway engine No. 2, 1922

By the end of World War I three railway lines jockeyed for business on the Saanich Peninsula. The always-marginal V&S operated with an annual subsidy from the City of Victoria. The City held bonds that financed the railway, and when they matured in 1919, there was no question of their renewal.

The closure marked the end of an era for Sidney, although Canadian National Railway bought the section between Bazan Bay and Sidney and used the line for transporting freight.

3. Sidney In Transition

Newlyweds Ed and Alice Renouf arrived in Sidney by car at 4 p.m. on Sunday, May 30, 1920, after immigrating from Guernsey Island, U.K. "Our first impressions," Ed reminisced in the *Islander* in 1981, "were that here was still an outpost of the far west."

"Early next morning we were out looking for a house. As today, housing was difficult to find. We struck it lucky and found a clean and tidy four-roomed house on 10 acres of mostly unproductive land, with a barn and a number of chicken houses. Not exactly cheap at $20 a month, but suitable for a start."

"There were few industries in the area. The Sidney Rubber Roofing was still operating, but the nearby iodine factory had closed and the shingle mill had burned down some time before. The salmon canney at Roberts Point had also closed, but the clam cannery near the wharf still operated in season. The lifeblood of Sidney was the sawmill – whenever it closed down for a couple of weeks it was a dull town."

Renouf, a gardener, quickly got a job at the Experimental Farm. Wages in Sidney were "anywhere from 25 to 32 cents an hour."

Harvest King

"With people settling down after overseas service, Sidney was now beginning to stir. Bill Stacey was opening a taxi service. Roy Brethour and Herman Shade were already established in a freight and milk service covering Sidney and North Saanich to Victoria. Other men were moving on to Soldier Settlement Farms."

Within two years of the Renoufs' arrival, the Great Northern dock was upgraded to cater to highway traffic between Vancouver Island and the United States mainland, and the little town began to nurture a new service industry. Car ferries are so familiar now, but front-loading vessels dedicated to vehicles were new in the 1920s. The MV *Harvester King*, one of the first ferries to operate between Sidney and Anacortes, was a converted kelp carrier that accommodated 12 cars. A turntable near the bow turned the vehicles around, and they backed in.

The car fare was $3 one-way and $5 return, while passengers paid $1. The American silver dollar in the corner of the photo was the first the ferry earned, and it took seven days! *Harvester King* and *Motor Princess*, the first true car ferry in the CPR Coast Steamship fleet, which opened the Sidney – Bellingham, Wa. route in 1923, were powered by diesel engines — and noisy, smoky, vibrating affairs they were. Internal combustion was inexorably pushing its way across land and sea, creating the world of the automobile that we so take for granted now.

The ungainly *Motor Princess*, dubbed The Galloping Dishpan, carried 45 cars and 250 passengers between Sidney and Bellingham. from 1923 to 1926, then was switched to the Nanaimo - Vancouver run. From 1929 to 1949 it linked Sidney with Steveston, at the mouth of the Fraser River, twice daily, and in 1933 Sunday tours of the Gulf Islands were added.

Forced out of service in 1949 by a ban on wooden-bodied vessels, she returned in 1956 with a steel superstructure, plying the short haul between Swartz Bay and Fulford Harbour, Salt Spring Island, for her new owner, the Gulf Islands Ferry Company.

The BC Ferry Corporation acquired the ferry and renamed her *Pender Queen* in 1963. After 1981, the old hull, so familiar in Sidney and North Saanich, took on a new life in remote settings as part of a deluxe fish camp.

The Motor Princess *unloading at Sidney's government dock.*

At the inauguration of the Sidney-Anacortes ferry in 1922, on the old wharf at the end of Second Street. Great Northern Railway's railcar barge dock, rebuilt for passenger ferries, was destroyed within 10 years. The Government of Canada built a new dock for the Washington State Ferry service in 1959.

Meanwhile, people in Sidney grasped the new opportunities. The Flying Line motor stage, whose driver Bill Landy is pictured at the front of this book, was established the year the V & S Railway passenger service to Sidney ceased. "All-red cars" made the trip to and from Victoria six times daily through the Twenties. The tall vehicle in the photo was the first bus in the area, according to historian Bea Bond: "Flying Line took a Cadillac chassis and built a new top on it. It had one passenger door, an aisle and two seats on either side. The body was lengthened — a nine- to 12-passenger vehicle. Leather top and glass windows." Other Flying Line cars had snap-on celluloid windows.

The period between the two world wars was transitional for Sidney in another way. As new ways of moving people and goods evolved, heavy industries on Vancouver Island found their transportation costs rising and their markets drying up. The withering of Sidney's smokestack industries accelerated with the closure for good of the sawmill in 1934.

THE GATEWAY TO VANCOUVER ISLAND, SIDNEY, B.C. CAN.

This wooden arch greeted ferry passengers arriving from the mainland during the Twenties.

The rumrunning fishpacker Beryl G *in Victoria*

Clam buying at the Sidney Government Dock, mid-1920s. Saanich Canning Company is on the L; the white building between the cannery and the Hotel Sidney was the town's original store; it was later added to the cannery. The building across the dock at R is the original Sidney Mills office. In 1939 C.C. Cochran and J.J. White sold the Saanich Cannery Company to BC Packers, who in turn sold it to Canadian Canners (Aylmer Brand). In the years of World War II, berry crops went to local wineries, and in 1942 the cannery closed forever. The cannery buildings were torn down in 1955.

Mayhem on the Straits

After the U.S. passed the Volstead Act in 1919, imposing prohibition on the sale of alcohol, Sidney became one of many rumrunning centres on Vancouver Island. Local runners ferried liquor across the straits to American ships, always under cover of night, employing complicated signals to establish bona fides without alerting customs officers. Up to 60 boats a night congregated at Discovery Island, off Victoria's east coast. In little coves and bays, serious money changed hands. There were stick-ups. There was murder.

In September 1924 a lightkeeper discovered the abandoned fishpacker *Beryl G* drifting off Stuart Island, about 16 km (10 mi) east of Sidney, decorated with blood stains and other signs of violence.

The British Columbia Police investigation traced the missing occupants — Vancouver fish packer William Gillis and his 17-year-old son Bill, Jr. — to a rumrunning operation. They delivered liquor from a freighter off the West Coast of Vancouver Island to a Seattle man who moored at Sidney, D'Arcy or Discovery islands.

Weeks turned into months before tips yielded two suspects in the disappearance: Harry Sowash and Owen Baker, American ex-cons who had preyed on rumrunners by posing as U.S. Customs agents. After an extensive search, Sowash and Baker were captured and returned to Victoria for trial. The accused claimed to have taken the *Beryl G's* liquor and dropped the occupants on a nearby islet.

Even though no trace of the Gillises was found, testimony by numerous individuals, including a third participant who turned Crown evidence, was enough to prove their evil deeds. The two had stalked the *Beryl G* inbound from its pick-up and boarded it off Sidney Island, under guise of the Law.

The elder Gillis, shotgun in hand, was killed almost at once. He and his son, knocked unconscious, were shackled together and thrown overboard. Moments later the crooks realized they had neglected to search Gillis's pockets for an estimated $3000 cash from an earlier sale! Baker and Sowash were executed January 1926.

The lounge at Resthaven

Resthaven Hospital served Sidney and North Saanich for more than 50 years. The fine building was gutted by fire while under construction on an island in All Bay in 1912. Intended as a club or lodge, it was briefly run as a 42-room sanatorium by Sidney doctor Gordon Cumming. During World War I it was a convalescent hospital for wounded soldiers. The Seventh Day Adventist Church bought the place in 1921 and, while, retaining its function as a restful seaside sanatorium, operated the Saanich Peninsula's first general hospital. A nursing school was attached to the hospital until 1936. Resthaven was granted full hospital status in 1949. A new hospital on Mt. Newton Cross Road opened in 1974, and Resthaven was torn down in 1978, making way for condominiums.

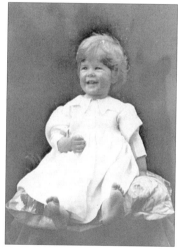

Enid F. Sisson was born in Resthaven Hospital on April 7, 1923 – the first child to see the light of day there.

The G.E. Goddard family moved from an Alberta Ranch into Captain Adamson's home and 10 acres on the windward side of Roberts Point in 1918. The property came to house the Goddard Chemical Company, maker of AK Boiler Fluids and other compounds — products used around the world to descale boilers (that is, remove minerals deposited on inside metal surfaces) in steam-powered ships and other steam-driven machines, including Sidney's own sawmill.

The Goddards had orchards and gardens, an Edwardian pavilion, a tennis court, a bathing house, a boathouse, an aviary and, attached to the house, a glassed-in verandah suitable for holding parties.

A son of the founder took over the business in 1930; more than five acres of the property was sold off, but the company continued to support the family (and a staff of two) until the last gasp of the steam era.

Today, grand-children live on the remnants of the Goddard estate. Surfside Place actually paved over part of the Goddards' tennis court, observes neighbour Cyril Hume, a Sidney heritage consultant.

J.B. Knowles delivered milk to Sidney-area residents for the Carnsew Dairy from 1910. Mr. Knowles retired this wagon in the 1920s and drove a Ford pick-up truck until retiring in 1942.

Road construction in Sidney, 1922. Bill Beswick is standing by the steamroller, and Ernie Munro is on the wagon.

The Sidney quarry, at the top of the Experimental Farm hill, provided the bed for the paving of the East Road.

Constructing the Swartz Bay road, June 1930. The East Road reached the north end of the Saanich Peninsula in a tiny forest clearing, where a new ferry dock accommodated a little ferry that shuttled to and from Fulford Harbour, on nearby Salt Spring Island.

A field of loganberry canes in Central Saanich, 1950s

Thomas and Lucy Lopthien established the first loganberry crops on the Saanich Peninsula about 1910. They purchased 100 tips from plant geneticist Luther Burbank and started them in an orchard on Roberts Bay. The loganberry is "thought to be a strain of either a variety of the Pacific dewberry (Rubus ursinus) or a hybrid between it and the red raspberry; the original plant appeared in the California orchard of Judge J. H. Logan in 1881" *(Columbia Encyclopedia)*.

These brambleberries grow on biannual canes, producing fruit every other year in tight clusters of drupelets that are larger and more tart than most of the bramble family. It took some years to get loganberries accepted in the jam, preserves and wine industries and, with the support of the Experimental Station, propagated throughout the peninsula. Tastes have changed, and today few loganberries are grown there.

Agriculture continues a mainstay of the Saanich Peninsula, even though Sidney has lost its connection with the industry, represented by this 1945 photo of the Saanich Fruitgrowers warehouse at Keating Cross Road and Veyaness Road, Central Saanich. Veyaness, as the name suggests, follows the old V&S Railway line, echoing Sidney's former status as the peninsula's processing and shipping centre

A raging inferno destroyed the fish reduction plant at Roberts Point in 1931. It was neither Sidney's first nor its last big fire. Sidney Rubber Roofing burned in 1921. The Berquist block, Beacon Avenue and Fourth Street, in January 1928, the North Saanich School in 1936, Sidney Hotel in 1948, Sandown Racetrack in 1966... The list goes on.

The Sidney Volunteer Fire Brigade was functioning by 1913. The firefighters would mobilize at a signal from the sawmill whistle and pull forest-fire fighting hoses on a cart to one of half a dozen hydrants. Then the men began to improvise serviceable fire vehicles out of an old Packard or a Cadillac. This rebuilt 1933 Ford truck - photographed during tests in 1945 - was truck No. 2. Also known as Old Betsy, she's a permanent resident among the thoroughly modern trucks and firefighting equipment at the Sidney Fire Hall, corner of Third Street and Sidney Avenue.

In the 1920s and '30s the Seagull Inn, at the corner of Beacon and Fourth, where Tanners Books now stands, was a boarding house, with attached café and bus depot.

In front of Stacey's hall and ice cream parlour, probably before 1930: George Wylie, Joe Musclow, Pat Clanton, S. Coward, Hugh Wylie and Jennie the horse, bearing Bill Lidgate.

Freeman King and Bob Boyd, leaders of work parties that put food on Sidney dinner tables in the depths of the Depression, at a Mt. Newton base camp.

Established in 1921 from the gift of a Mt. Newton property owner, John Dean Park was the first area in B.C. donated to the Crown for protection. Freeman King, a native of England, settled with his family in Sidney in 1925 and went to work for Sidney Lumber. A scouting enthusiast, King soon started leading troops of kids on excursions around still-wild parts of the peninsula. Appointed to head the Dean Park administration board in 1934, "Skipper" King and the Sidney Scout Troop built many trails across the forested slopes of Mt. Newton. The B.C. Forest Service hired King in 1937. Bob Boyd was foreman of a forest service training crew that built the road from the East Road into the park in 1938 for access in case of fire and constructed many amenities — picnic sites, a dam, well-masoned walls, the gate posts at the park entrance, a stone staircase — in use today.

The Piers Penitentiary

In April 1932 more than 600 Doukhobor followers of the Christian Community of Universal Brotherhood, a communal sect of Russian origin living in the West Kootenay region, were charged with publicly disrobing to protest the imprisonment of their leader, Peter Verigin.

Sentenced to three years in prison, they were accommodated at a minimum security penitentiary constructed for the purpose on Piers Island, while their children were placed in orphanages and foster homes around Victoria, Vancouver and the Lower Mainland. From November 1932, when the first prisoners were transported to the 98-hectare (241-acre) island, just west of Swartz Bay, until March 1935, when the last inmates were released, the island resounded with the Douhobors' devotional singing.

The island was restored to its former owners, resold, subdivided into 129 waterfront lots, marketed as summer cottage properties, which proved popular. A 1966 ode by Mary Bain captures the sentiments of a generation of summer cottagers. It begins thus:

> *I long for the years of a life on Piers*
> *Where the Pacific's blue waters play,*
> *An island retreat that cannot be beat,*
> *For a lengthy and wonderful stay....*

Reefnetting

Like other Straits Salish nations, the Saanich people use this team technique of corraling schooled salmon as they return to their rivers of origin to spawn. Washington ethnologist Wayne Suttles deemed the practise "of paramount importance in the aboriginal economy of the Straits peoples." It was discontinued from the mid-1890s, when "most of the better reef-netting grounds in the state of Washington were blocked by traps," until 1934, when the traps were removed by law, prompting "a considerable revival."

Most of the Saanich chiefs' reef-netting rights were located around Point Roberts, on the mainland side of the Strait of Georgia. This photo, taken by Clifford Carl of the BC Provincial Museum in 1951, shows Saanich fishers south of Reid Harbour on Stuart Island, using reef-nets to catch sockeye migrating north on Haro Strait.

Typically, the chief put a team together in June, established a summer camp near the place and, at the lowest tide in June, set anchors on the seafloor. On a flood tide, huge nets attached to the anchors were pulled upcurrent by a pair of large wooden boats fitted with platforms, where observers could follow the fish.

Aboriginal fishers reef-netting salmon.

Cars waiting to board Cy Peck *at Swartz Bay in the 1940s. Captain George Maud took passengers' fares on the dock, then climbed to the wheelhouse to skipper the ship. The* Cy Peck, *the former ss Island Princess, was bought by the Gulf Island Ferry Company in 1930 and refitted with diesel engines. She served on the Swartz Bay - Fulford Harbour run for more than a quarter century.*

Beached Minke whale in front of Eva Williams' house, 2532 Beaufort Road, 1940. Joe Musclow, at R, worked for the Sidney Review

Patricia Bay Airport

Battered by the Depression, Sidney's salvation came from the air — literally – when Canada's Department of Transport chose North Saanich as the site of air training bases and a military airport in 1937, under gathering war clouds. The needed 700 acres of nice flat land were appropriated and three bases were constructed, with common runways and control tower.

More than 10,000 airmen and servicewomen flooded into North Saanich. They were greeted with open arms. By day and night the skies buzzed with Liberators, Lancasters and Bolingbrokes, Mosquitoes and Curtiss Kittyhawks. Mary's Coffee Bar, on the nearby East Road, vibrated with talk and music on the jukebox, 24 hours a day. Sidney prospered again.

The year it opened, Patricia Bay was the third largest air station in Canada. At West Camp, on the west side of the peninsula, lodged the Royal Canadian Air Force's operational training unit (OTU) No. 3. The Royal Canadian Navy had a seaplane base on the nearby bay. East Camp, was occupied by the Royal Air Force's OTU No. 31.

The RCAF base at Patricia Bay. Long after the war, the recreation hall, L, was touted as a community hall for Sidney. The town eventually built its own, and this building was demolished in 1958.

Some 3500 personnel were enrolled in the Commonwealth Training Program at any time, including pilots, navigators, machine gunners, ground control, maintenance and mechanical crews. The air forces of Australia and New Zealand participated. The OTU's trained more than 850 pilots in all.

Patricia Bay Airport also housed an elementary flying school and, after Pearl Harbour, a base for reconnaissance bombers and fighter units. The human cost of this operation was surprisingly high. During the war some 100 airborne lives were lost because of accident, error or mechanical misadventure. The worst was in 1942, when a Liberator went down in Sansum Narrows, killing 11 people. A plaque at Victoria International Airport commemorates the loss.

The early history of the airport is memorialized at the B.C. Aviation Museum, housed in the old East Camp, at 1910 Norseman Road. The high-octane life of the wartime Pat Bay station was featured, improbably, in the 1943 Hollywood film *Son of Lassie*. Scenes from the movie were included in Sidney's 1991 commemorative video.

Squadron Leader Connel poses beside his fighter with his mascot dog Queenie during World War II

Westland "Lysander" bombers at Patricia Bay, 1942

The Canso "Flying Boat" crew at the RCAF Marine Station, Patricia Bay, 1943

An RAF reception at Patricia Bay

The U.S. Navy blimp King 79 at Patricia Bay, April 1944

A DC3 on the tarmac at the Patricia Bay airport, 1947.

Trans-Canada Air Lines (TCA) began service between Victoria and Seattle in 1939, but until 1943 Canadian Pacific Air Lines had the licence to fly passengers between Victoria and Vancouver. TCA service to Vancouver began that year with two flights a day in a 14-passenger Lockheed. Civilian services began to use the East Camp (pictured here) in 1947.

In May 1948, airport administration reverted to Transport Canada. The RCAF presence lingered until 1952. The name was changed to Victoria International Airport in 1959. The present terminal, on the south side of the airport, dates from 1964.

Renovation beginning in 1985 doubled the size of the building. The East -West runway was lengthened to 7,000 ft (2134 m) in stages between 1961 and 1971 to handle full-sized passenger jets — cutting off the East Road in the process. A connector road was completed to shorten access between Sidney and the airport.

The airport now encompasses 482 hectares and is leased to the Victoria Airport Authority, established in 1997.

Passengers boarding a TCA plane, 1946

The Saanich Peninsula grew seasonal spring flowers, and commercial airlines shipped them to market — et voilà! daffodils and tulips for Easter in snowy Montreal.

Irene Henderson and Jerry Gosley playing to Commonwealth troops near the line in Korea in 1952, with Al Denoni on accordian.

Jerry Gosley's Smile Show

Yorkshire-born Jerry Gosley (1916-1996) apprenticed as a printer and worked in the newspaper trade. In 1939 he tried to enlist with the Royal Air Force but was diagnosed variously with an enlarged heart, poor eyesight and a stammer. After Dunkirk, he was accepted for ground crew and put on wireless training. Gosley's company shipped out, landed in Halifax, crossed Canada and fetched up at the Patricia Bay RAF training base. They found "no big aerodrome, no hangars, no control tower, no planes, only fields and a cluster of big barrack huts".

Gosley was appalled. Patricia Bay's pastoral setting was no picnic for nearly 2000 "idle, despondent men" whose families back home were getting bombed out of their homes. Gosley started a base newsletter, The Patrician, financing its publication by selling ads.

Asserting his experience in amateur dramatics, Gosley was put in charge of organizing "station concert parties" — variety shows. These popular events, which came to be called Smile Shows, gave morale a

76

boost. They played in Victoria. The troupe got leave to travel, and the Smile Show proved a hit in the Seattle area, too.

When a film shoot for a Hollywood propaganda movie, *The Commandos Strike at Dawn*, came to Patricia Bay in the summer of 1942, Gosley invited the stars to appear at a Smile Show. "Paul Muni refused, but Sir Cedric Hardwicke, his charming wife Helena, Lilian Gish and Robert Coote all came." Gosley's 1964 biography, *Nowhere Else to Go*, relates that RAF airmen, drafted as extras for the film and dressed as German soldiers, disgraced themselves on their first day by stealing the medals and were replaced by soldiers.

Re-posted to England, Gosley auditioned for the Gang Shows that gave Peter Sellers and Tony Hancock their start in show business. He spent the heady post-War months touring the Mediterranean with the show, then returned to the printer's trade, marrying Peggy Gregg, the bookkeeper at his workplace. Before long Jerry convinced Peg they should move to the Saanich Peninsula. After getting a sponsor for immigration (a Smile Show alumnus from Pat Bay), they arrived in Sidney in 1947 and scrabbled for a living. She opened Peg's Pantry, a bakery-deli on Beacon Avenue. They would jig for cod on Sunday afternoons and make fishcakes that evening for sale on Monday.

Soon they moved to Victoria, where Jerry built a printing business. Meanwhile, Gosley contacted former Smile Show people, found new talent and put together a show. They toured Korea in 1952. The Smile Show was often sponsored by the Canadian Legion to entertain service people, such as those at isolated air force bases in Tofino and Holberg. Other performances were mounted in cancer clinic, tuberculosis ward or solarium.

In the early 1960s, the Smile Show turned commercial and was a summertime hit in Victoria until the late 1970s. It was last revived in 1997, to create a bursary for young performing artists.

Nowhere Else to Go (published in Sidney by Gray's Publishing) describes one of Gosley's favorite opening bits: a pompous British twit in a blue blazer clamps his eye around a monocle, surveys the audience "with fatuous benevolence" and drawls, "I'm awfully glad to be heah." Pause. "I'd nowhere else to go."

The Sidney and North Saanich Community Hall Association (SANSCHA) was formed in 1953 to get a community centre going. The original scheme was to move the recreation hall at Patricia Bay Airport to War Memorial Park, south of Beacon Avenue in what was then countryside. SANSCHA decided to build a new hall from scratch. Contractor Andries Boas donated weeks of his time to supervise the building's construction. Six carpenters worked for wages, and many residents volunteered their labour. Supplies and other costs were financed by floating debentures. Most creditors later tore up their debentures. SANSCHA Hall is the town's most visible landmark from the Patricia Bay Highway. Owned since 1964 by the North Saanich Memorial Park Trust — whose members include all North Saanich and Sidney residents — the hall and its grassy surroundings have become hot property. Arterial development has already shaved land off the sides and front of the park. During one modification, the war memorial itself was summarily uprooted from consecrated ground and removed to Sidney municipal grounds.

SANSCHA Hall under construction, 1957-58

The May Queen and attendants at a Sidney celebration in the late 1940s.

Sidney Days, 1958

Sidney Hospitality

In 1958, the centennial of British Columbia's establishment as a Crown colony, the province's growing tourist industry was bedevilled by labour-management conflict. A strike by one of the Canadian Pacific Steamships' three labour unions stopped all passenger service between Victoria and Vancouver in May. When Black Ball Ferry workers went on strike on July 18, Vancouver Island lost all connection with the B.C. mainland, leaving only the two ferries from Victoria to Port Angeles and from Sidney to Anacortes in operation.

Hundreds of vehicles descended on Sidney, and for five days the little village was swamped. As North Saanich publisher Gray Campbell told it in a 1961 *Islander* article, the community mobilized quickly to prevent chaos on the streets of the still-small village (pop: 1,500).

On that hot Friday morning, Beacon was already "full of cars to the edge of the business district, and it was obvious that before the next ferry it would be plugged to the corner [of East Saanich Road] and then far back down the highway. That is if drivers looking for short cuts didn't create a colossal traffic jam."

For decades, cars lined up in the middle of Beacon Avenue to wait for the ferry, as in this photo from the late 1940s

Norman Wright, the Standard Oil agent in Sidney, organized a team of volunteers to clear Beacon and re-form the line-up on the grassy grounds of War Memorial Park, giving each car a number. Civil Defence volunteer co-ordinator Gwyn Owen mustered an auxiliary police force that directed new arrivals.

Betty Eckert, having recently organized the food for Sidney Day, took time off from Sidney Dry Goods to take charge of provisioning the horde. Volunteer helpers sold hot dogs, chips, soft drinks — any fast food they could obtain at local grocery stores — at cost. Phyllis Levar set up an accommodation service that solicited billets by telephone and even loud-speaker. The army garrison in Victoria sent out two trucks with 600 pairs of blankets. An entertainment committee showed films on a 16-mm projector and organized square dances "for the younger people."

Ferries loaded up into the night. The fire-chief's vehicle, roof-light flashing, led slow cavalcades."All through the night cars arrived, and were sorted, instructed, accommodated. Some slept in the hall, upstairs and down, some in cars, some in tents and others around town. Dawn found teams from the Rotary Club and the Legion on the grounds, making breakfast. "

"A group from the Victoria Chamber of Commerce arrived. The situation in Victoria was awful. They were getting bad publicity. Tourists were parked on the streets. They could not leave their cars or get food. There was no accommodation. The police were giving them tickets for holding their places in line. Loud were the complaints."

After the last ferry left Sidney on the second day, 500 cars remained. No problem. The community effort expanded. Young people who liked to fix up old cars went around filling gas tanks and servicing vehicles — you just put your hood up or turned on your lights. On Sunday, church-goers were escorted to local services. Families offered sight-seeing drives and trips to nearby beaches.

An estimated 7,000 people, stranded for at least a day, returned to Ontario or California with vivid impressions of a small town most hadn't planned to visit and many had never heard of. The town's hospitality and community spirit were featured in newsapers as far away as Hong Kong.

Boat building, Canoe Cove, about 1954.

The longest-lived boat builder in the Sidney area, is Canoe Cove Manufacturing. In the 1920s the Copeland & Wright marine ways and machine shop, now long-vanished, stood by the old V&S wharves, just south of the Saanich Canning plant. Another centre of the industry is at All Bay, on the south side of Tsehum (Shoal) Harbour, while Philbrook's yard, off Harbour Road, has been making custom diesel yachts since the 1950s. Brent Jespersen worked there before setting up his own yard, catering to the laminated wood sailboat market.

Today, a host of custom builders and designers work out of Sidney. Many are attached to the marinas. The busiest boat-building centre in British Columbia, Sidney has an international reputation.

Commercial fishboat Ocean Producer *was launched in 1964 — the last wooden-hulled boat made at Canoe Cove Manufacturing.*

Picnic at Sidney Spit Marine Provincial Park, 1960. Sidney Island, 9.5 km long and 800 ha in area, was the site of a brick factory from 1906 to 1916, later a game preserve for well-heeled Victoria-area families. The BC Government bought 80 hectares in 1960 and created this popular park. Sidney Spit is the narrow neck of sand at the northern tip of the island. A walk-on ferry transports visitors from Sidney in season.

Motor boat moored off Sidney Spit, 1959

The newly-completed Patricia Bay Highway (BC Highway 17), north of Island View Road, in Central Saanich, early 1950s.

This picture captures the last days of the old order on the Saanich Peninsula. Before the 1960s, its strongly agricultural communities lived in relative seclusion, relatively self-sufficiently. The centres were tiny. There was little industry. The Patricia Bay Highway, for which surveys began in 1948-49, extended Victoria's Douglas Street north to Royal Oak; East Saanich Road was upgraded between the Royal Oak intersection with West Saanich Road and Keating Cross Road; and a new segment used railway grade north of Keating, intersecting the East Road near the old airport centre. The "Pat Bay" Highway was destined not for Patricia Bay, as the name suggests, but to the airport of the same name. Fortuitously, the highway did come to terminate in a bay. In 1960 a new stretch of Highway 17 opened between McTavish Road and Swartz Bay to provide access to the BC Ferries terminal. The expropriated right-of-way cut a swathe through the farmland east of the airport, much of it still the property of North Saanich and Sidney pioneering families. Enlarged repeatedly as traffic multiplied, the Pat Bay Highway and the Swartz Bay terminal have reshaped Sidney, segregating its coastal and inland sides and adding fuel to the growth that has changed the face of the town.

Sidney *launched at the Victoria Machinery Depot, near Ogden Point, Victoria on October 6, 1959*

Following the ferry workers' strike in 1958, the government of W.A.C. Bennett created the British Columbia Ferry Corporation. The first ships were named *Sidney* and *Tsawwassen* — "Queen of" was prefixed later. They were modelled on *Coho*, which docks in Victoria harbour, in front of the B.C. Parliament Buildings. Legend has it that highways minister Phil Gaglardi, responsible for the creation of this provincial "navy," looked out his office window in the Parliament Buildings, saw *Coho* and told his engineers to design a similar vessel.

When the BC Government chose the site of the little ferry dock built in 1930 as the terminus of a new service to the mainland shore near Tsawwassen, south of Vancouver, it fulfilled a vision propounded in 1886 by Victoria legislator Amor de Cosmos.

It seems to work. The terminal now handles some seven million passengers a year bound to or from Tsawwassen.

The Swartz Bay ferry terminal under construction in June 1960, Sidney *and* Tsawwassen *at berth. In this photo, Canoe Cove is at top centre.*

4. Sidney's Heritage Today

"An absence from fogs and the rougher winds, and a degree of sunshine almost unknown on this favored coast, make the district peculiarly fitted to be chosen as a seaside and health resort. The surpassing beauty of the surrounding bays and islands, and their dainty and welcoming shore lines, will make Sidney more attractive every year to the world at large, and tourists in increasing numbers may be expected to favor this place with their very best regards and yearly attentions." — *"Sidney's Sanatorium," in the Sidney and Islands Review, first issue, September 13, 1912*

"I have always believed, and still believe, that the Saanich Peninsula is destined to become wholly residential." — *J.J. White, in the* Review, *1952.*

One didn't need a crystal ball to see Sidney's destiny, even in the early years. As for the town's recent history, we need not consult old photographs and clippings. It's still happening. We can experience it first-hand on the street.

Among the trends:

The population is up dramatically, from 3,000 at the time of Sidney's incorporation as a town, in 1967, to just over 11,000 in 1997.

North Saanich has become the major corridor between Victoria and Vancouver. (The comparatively tiny Sidney-Anacortes ferry service is, however, in danger of folding.)

The international airport is busier than ever.

Marine traffic in pleasure craft is also up markedly.

Sidney's service industries have expanded to serve the emerging bedroom community and the expanded highway and marine trades.

Sidney is rich in many ways, but not in its historic remains. They can be surveyed in little more than an hour, studied in a day.

Here's a quick tour of Sidney's heritage artifacts, buildings and museums.

Central

A good place to start is on the pier at the foot of Beacon Avenue. To the south is a new fishing pier; to the north, the extensive Port of Sidney development and breakwater. While the breakwater dates only from 1989 it rates as an historical attraction, since its construction has been on the agenda since at least 1912. The goal was always to establish public moorage on Sidney's exposed southern coastline, buffeted by southeasterly winds. Though the $3.2-million breakwater was publicly funded, the moorage remains private. Lively discussion attends the mere mention of the word "breakwater."

The Sidney Museum, 9801 Seaport Place, has a small, well-displayed suite of historical artifacts and family history, sharing the enlarged old Customs Building with a marine mammal display. The picture above shows a line-up on the dock at the foot of Beacon in 1950. Vehicles from the United States would drive through the Customs Building (centre background). The museum was established in 1971, courtesy of a large donation by Mary and Joe John.

The Mitchell and Anderson lumber store, at the northeast corner of Beacon and Second, was pulled down in July 1981, and with it went Sidney's connection with the sawmill. It's now the site of the Landmark Building. The anchor bolt in the sidewalk outside the building is all that remains of Sidney's sawmilling past. It secured one of several guylines that held up the mill's derrick. The plaque commemorates the mill.

The Sidney Post Office, 2423 Beacon Avenue, was built in 1936. It was the first building in Sidney to get heritage designation. Here, bike racers pose in 1937.

This 1948 view down Beacon Avenue shows Frank's News, at the corner of Fourth Street — now Tanners, a Bookstore and More, 2436 Beacon Avenue. The Star Weekly sign hung there until 1988 and now resides in the BC Sign Museum.

Mason's Exchange, Plumbing and Electric Store, Beacon Avenue, west of Fifth Street, about 1933 or '34. Children from L: Ben Wells, Leslie Stirling, Masoa Baba, Cootie, Dave Stirling, Jim Mason, Skiddo and Gordon Manning. The building, originally a barn, became an antique store and is now Beacon Books, a vintage book and paper collectibles store.

South

Mary's has operated for six decades at 9535 Canora (previously East Saanich) Road. Among its trove of memorabilia is this photograph from the 1930s, showing Sidney - Victoria buses outside the tiny cafe.

The unusual Brethour family cemetery, at the corner of Ocean Avenue and Canora Road, was established in 1885 and is a designated heritage site

North

One of a number of fine houses in the northern part of Sidney, Miraloma was the summer residence of Vancouver publisher Walter C. Nichol, the province's Lieutenant Governor from 1920 to 1926, and his family. Nichol commissioned Victoria architect Samuel Maclure to design a rustic retreat on 19 acres at Thumb Point. The distinctive bark-clad exterior of the house has become well-known since the place, much reduced in area and surrounded by suburban development, was converted to an up-scale restaurant, The Latch. It's now The Latch Country Inn, 2328 Harbour Road, a spiffy five-unit lodge.

This beautiful Craftsman residence on Beaufort Road was built in 1915 by Stanley Brethour for the C.C. Cochran family. (Visitors to Roberts Point and other heritage enclaves in Sidney should respect the right of property owners to privacy and be aware of limited on-street parking.)

Acknowledgements

For assistance in gaining access to archival photographs in the Sidney Museum, many thanks to Peter Garnham and Sherry Easthom, and to the Town of Sidney; many thanks also to Laurette Agnew, Frank Kennell and other members of the Saanich Pioneers' Society; to life member Harry Nunn of the Sidney Volunteer Fire Department; and to staff at BC Archives and the Royal BC Museum.

Thanks to individuals who loaned their precious prints.

For assistance with historical content, thanks to Moran Brethour; to Norman Wright; to Darryl Muralt; to Cyril Hume; to Grant Keddie and Alan Hoover, Royal BC Museum; and to Jim Alsbury, Centre for Plant Health.

For permission to use excerpts from published books, thanks to Darryl E. Muralt and Gray Campbell. The account of the sinking of the *Iroquois* is from Muralt's *V&S: The Victoria and Sidney Railway 1892-1919* (B.C. Railway Historical Association, 1992). The rumrunning tale was documented in The Beryl G Mystery by Cecil Clark in *The Daily Colonist*, May 5 and 12, 1957. The story of the Piers Island Penitentiary and the excerpt of ode are from *Piers Island* by A. Harold Skolrood (1995). Ed Renouf's description of Sidney is taken from the *Islander*, August 2-4, 1981. The biographical sketch of Jerry Gosley was adapted from *Nowhere Else To Go* by John Windsor (Sidney, Gray's Publishing, 1964). Gray Campbell's account of the 1958 ferry strike was published in *The Daily Colonist*, May 7, 1961.

Special thanks to Moran Brethour, Darryl Muralt, Brad Morrison and Norman Wright for reviewing manuscript.

For the concept and the encouragement, thanks to my publishers.

To the people of Sidney and the Saanich Peninsula who keep the lamps of local history and heritage alight, this book is dedicated.

Photo credits

Sidney Museum: cover, 1, 2, 5, 18, 21 top (t), 23 (all), 25 t, 26, 28, 29 b, 30-31, 32 t, 33 b, 34 t+b, 37, 38 t, 39 t, 40 t+b, 41 b, 42 t+b, 43 t+b, 44, 46, 47, 50 t+b, 54 t+b, 55, 58 t+b, 60 t+b, 61 t+b, 62 t, 63, 64 t, 65 t+b, 69 b, 70, 71, 72 t, 73 t, 79 t+b, 80, 84 t, 89, 90 b, 91 t+b, 93, 94

Saanich Pioneers' Society: 6, 21 b, 22 t (both), 27, 32 b, 38-39, 56 b

Darryl E. Muralt: 9, 51

Royal BC Museum: 10 (PN7201), 11 (PN13454.19), 12 (PN818), 13 (PN5918), 14t (PN7786), 14b (PN6832), 68 (PN11359)

BC Archives: 16 (HP532), 17 (HP33711), 19 (HP25783), 20 (HP3183), 22 b (HP68688), 25 b (HP54362), 29 t (HP70161), 33 t (HP49456), 35 t (HP78129) 35 b (HP34827), 36 (HP49452), 41 t (HP61844), 45 (HP85996), 48 (HP55112), 49 (HP23840), 52 (HP79076), 56 t (HP38542), 62 b (HP9159), 67 (HP72168), 69 t (A33), 72 b (G04113), 73 b (HP96888), 74 (MCP4029), 75 t (B03-A0352), 75 b (B03-A0355), 82 (HP74092), 84 b (B03-00165), 85 (I-26706), 86 (HP86517), 87 (HP77927)

Hugh Godwin: 59

Sidney Volunteer Fire Department: 64 b

Jarrett Teague: 66

Al Denoni: 76

Andries Boas: 78

Don Matheson: 83

Peter Grant: 90 t, 92 b

Mary's Bleue Moon Café: 92 t

Molly Grant: 96

Peter Grant is a native of Vancouver Island. He has published hundreds of articles on history, geography, forestry, travel and other regional subjects, and is the author of a guide book, Victoria from Sidney to Sooke (1994), and the companion Victoria a History in Photographs (1995). He lives in Victoria with Paula and their daughter Molly.